C000183239

Contents

Acknowledgements

Our gratitude goes to: Mike Baker, Denise Banwell, John Batt, Pat Brain, Revd J.A. Braine, T. Howard Butler, Roy Clevely, John Cornwall, Mrs Dale, Mr T.J. Dart, Peter Davey, Richard Davis, Mrs H. Daunton, Mr Dring, Mrs Flay, Sydney Gamblin, Rita Garland, Pam Gear, Mr W. Gunningham, David Harrison, Clive Hobbs, Jean Hobbs, Norman Hobbs, Brian Hodges, Vera Hodges, Edward Jackson, David Lambert, C.G. Lewis, Jim McNeill, Ray Morgan, David Norman, Andy Parsons, Joyce Peters, Delores Powell, Mr H.B. Priestley, Oscar Rees, Mr G.W Roberts, Iris Royston, Ken Smith, F.H. Stevens, Joseph Stratford, Paul Tompsett, M.J. Tozer, Bristol Records Office, Bristol City Council, Bristol Evening Post, Bristol Central Library, St George Library, St George School, Bethesda Church, St Patrick's Church.

Special thanks to: Tony Brake, Ivor Cheesley, Jean Cheesley, Susan Davis, Ernie Haste, Molly Foss, Leslie Furnivall, Reg Gregory, Dorothy Jones, John Merrett, Kath Nurse, Doreen Parsons, William Sanigar, Dennis Stephenson.

Introduction

A Brief History of the Parish of St George

In olden days, the eastern approach to the City of Bristol was dominated by the extensive Forest of Kingswood (once a royal preserve) and two ancient tracks: the London and Bath roads. St George at the time of the Norman Conquest was part of the Manor of Bertune. The King's Barton, or farm, stretched from Bristol Castle to the Forest of Kingswood. The forest, home to deer and other game, was also home, from the medieval period, to the mining of coal. In stark contrast to this underground pursuit, families began farming the land of the area at a similar time.

At the exit from the Forest of Kingswood, at the Bristol end, was the site of the fabled Don John's Cross. At this point, later occupied by the Fountain, the two roads through the forest merged to form one vital communication artery leading to Bristol. It was adjacent to this road fork that St George Church was consecrated in 1756, a significant event in the history of the area. Created from the division of the parish of St Philip Jacob in 1751, the new church gave its name to the surrounding district.

From the heights of the forest, the road, cited in 1756 as the 'Turnpike Road from Bristol to Marshfield', dropped down as it stretched west. It was bordered by a patchwork of fields, a result of the land enclosure which took place between 1400 and 1600. The business of market gardening became firmly established in the area, as the land was well suited to this occupation. Vegetables and fruit were grown for sale in Bristol's markets and for local consumption. Families such as the Leonards, Gerrishes, Johnsons and Phipps successfully cultivated a large number of fields, overlooked by their homestead and outbuildings. In other fields the development of steam-powered machinery allowed deep shafts to tap into the east Bristol coalfield. These replaced the earlier shallow workings. It was in fields adjacent to these pits that Whitefield and Wesley preached to colliers of the area. The subsequent development of Methodism was to have a significant impact on the area.

In the early nineteenth century, the Wain Brook flowed past the parish poor workhouse, while narrow rough paths led from the road. Pitch-dark by night, annuls of recorded crime show that it was unsafe to travel alone by night. Ranks of cottages were built to house the ever increasing population of the area. Although, in contrast were the large estates such as Redfield House and Whitehall House. These revolved around large and elegant houses set in extensive grounds and with assorted supporting buildings.

The gradual urbanization of the area was a consequence of the industrial revolution and the resulting Victorian expansion of Bristol. The City Boundary was not extended until 1897, but as early as 1874 the St George Local Board was created. This was an important event for the area, reflecting the growth and prosperity of St George. The area covered by the Board was quite extensive: from the Feeder at Barton Hill to Clay Hill and across to parts of Kingswood and Conham Vale. With wide powers, and led by some visionary and influential figures, the St George Local Board was to take some bold steps in its twenty-three years of existence.

From the 1870s onwards, there was a steady drift away from market gardening in the Redfield area. The landowners moved out, selling their land to speculative builders, eager to satisfy the increasing demand for houses. Plots of land were disposed of gradually as the estates were whittled down. This process happened in a piecemeal, gradualist manner, in the days before the town and country planning system. Parts of Whitehall in the 1920s for example, still had fields where rows of lettuce and spring onions were grown. In the main, meadows were replaced by variations of the 'villa style' terraced house. These reflected new bylaws designed to secure proper standards of drainage as well as regulate the size of rooms and the width of the street.

By 1900, key community features were in place. Imposing Board schools and churches had been built. An increasing and varied selection of shops emerged to serve the ever growing number of households. Small to medium-sized businesses grew, while brick factories were built. These new buildings joined the inns and taverns of the area, some of which had stood for hundreds of years. Mining was to remain a factor in the area until the 1920s and '30s. As well as the pits, the northern part of St George also had quarries, brick and tile producers and the Atlas locomotive works. At the opposite end of the district, Butler's tar works together with St Anne's Board Mills, dominated the industry of the Crews Hole valley.

By the start of the First World War, most of Redfield, Whitehall and lower St George had been built up. The next expansion would be in St George East, moving toward Kingswood and Hanham. In the 1920s this was still an area of farms, old quarry workings, allotment gardens and a maze of quaintly named footpaths and fields. Many houses were subsequently built in the period before the Second World War. Nurseries, glasshouses, and cottages vanished in the process. Significantly the fields around the Fire Engine Farm escaped the builders and were moulded into an elaborate showcase by St George Council. The resulting St George Park has been a popular playground for local people for over 100 years.

The district evolved throughout the nineteenth and twentieth centuries, with a mix of characteristic shops, schools, churches, factories and pubs. These served and were part of the community and life of the people of St George, Redfield and Whitehall.

One

Early Days

An Act of Parliament decreed that St George Parish must build its own poorhouse, maintain its own poor and repair its own highways and a poorhouse was opened in 1801. Thomas Thurston of Whitehall was one of the commissioners. It was later taken over by the Clifton Poor Law Union when the area came into the boundary of Bristol. The poorhouse was used for housing pauper children.

From 1869 to 1904 the structure was part of the Crown Pottery Co. It was owned by the Ellis family who also ran the Victoria Pottery in St Philips Marsh. Later it was owned by Pountneys before they built their Fishponds factory.

The old poorhouse then began to be used for a number of industrial purposes. It was a leather warehouse and then a soap factory owned by J.L. Thomas. A big fire, plus intense competition, closed this concern down. In the 1920s R. Moon and Co. made decorative tins at the site, as did Avon tin who followed them. Avon Tin was of great renown, selling tins all over the world. They moved to Station Road, Kingswood, in the 1970s. Various businesses used the old site including Glenfrome Engineering, who customized and stretched cars to make limousines. Today the old poorhouse building still remains but the Wainbrook which once ran alongside it is well hidden underground.

The building that was once St George poorhouse.

The base of Don John's Cross. In 2000 the remains of the famous cross were placed on this plinth outside St George library. Whether, as some think, the cross commemorated a Spanish nobleman or was instead a boundary marker for Kingswood Forest ('Dungeon Cross'), the legend of Don John's Cross has been associated with the area for hundreds of years.

Don John's Cross public house.

Redfield House, a substantial property built in the eighteenth century. The house was set within extensive grounds comprising of landscaped gardens, paddocks and fields. A range of outbuildings, including stables and a brew-house, served the estate. In 1831 Lt-Col. Brereton, in charge of the troops in the Bristol Riots, committed suicide in the house. Demolished in 1899, the site of the main house is now occupied by Verrier and Weight Roads.

George and Dragon Lane. Indicated on the 1845 Tithe Map of the area, it ran from Church Road to Pilemarsh and was mainly built over in 1972 when Vetchlea elderly people's home was built.

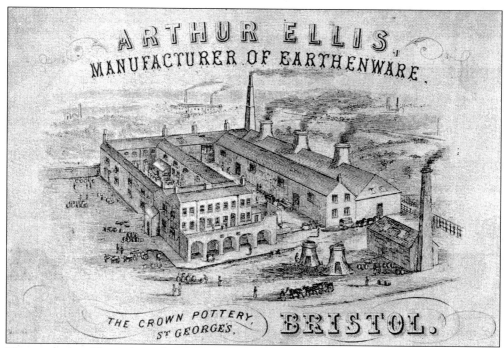

The poorhouse. This is the earliest known drawing of the old St George poorhouse. At this time it was the Crown Pottery, owned by Arthur Ellis (1869-1904).

The milestone on Summerhill Road which dates from around 1800. This is a diagonally set stone at the entrance to a lane which leads to Troopers Hill. Its 'two-face' design is unusual and notable.

Summerhill House: a much loved building now demolished. This fine house was built on land that was part of the estate of Thomas Masters. The house became the home of William Henry Butler, son of William Butler (founder of tar works), in the 1860s. In 1925 the house was occupied by Dr Edwin F. Foss, in 1940 by Dr George L. Foss and in the 1950s by Dr Joan Mary Foss and her husband Dr Struthers. The house was demolished in the early 1960s, two ranks of new houses were built and Summerhill Road was widened.

Homefield House: the residence of the Emra family. In 1830 Elizabeth Emra wrote the book *Scenes in our Parish by a Country Parson's daughter*. In this narrative she gave glimpses of her favourite St George retreats. The house, across from the vicarage of St George Church, was demolished in the 1990s.

Thurstons Barton. The seventeenth and eighteenth centuries saw an increase in the number of workers cottages in the area. Usually built in small ranks, often alongside 'bartons'. Another example was Gingell's Barton, off of Two Mile Hill Road. Some of these old cottages survived until the 1960s and '70s.

Thurstons Barton, Whitehall. On this narrow lane, leading from Whitehall Road, Thomas Thurston erected a number of cottages in the eighteenth century. Some survived, such as the ones next to Rose Green School, into the 1970s. Adjacent to the Barton was the site where Wesley and Whitefield preached to the masses. In 1739 it was known as the Crabtree Ground. This delightful lane and surrounding greenery was covered by new houses from 1986 onwards.

Gerrish House on the corner of Gilbert Road and Whitehall Road, an elegant country house dating from around 1770. The house was part of the Gerrish estate of market gardens and orchards. In the 1870s it became the vicarage for St Gabriel's Church. The Gerrish family's other residence, Cambridge House was next door.

Cambridge House, home to the Gerrish family. The back faced onto Gilbert Road, while Gerrish Avenue and Samuel Street were built to the front of the house. There were a number of adjoining outbuildings including glasshouses and, in the 1950s, a row of garages. All were demolished in July 1964 and replaced by a rank of houses.

Devon House, an impressive early nineteenth-century house, now offices, on the corner of Devon and Whitehall Roads. This was Dr Cairns house for many years who was a respected Whitehall figure. In the nineteenth century the area to the south-east of the house, the Albert Parade area, was known as 'The Wilderness'. Here the Wainbrook passed through a gorse gully and headless ghosts were reputed to roam!

The Limes, on the corner of Johnson Lane, Whitehall. Originally the residence of Mr Johnson, a prominent market gardener, it was, at that time, surrounded by an impressive fully enclosed garden. After the Johnsons vacated, it was home to the manager of Packers chocolate factory. It has been a nursery school for many years.

THE
LIMES NURSERY
SCHOOL

Holly Lodge House was situated in a picturesque location between Deep Pit and Speedwell Pit. It was the residence of Handel Cossham MP, the prominent Liberal and non-conformist colliery owner (see p. 99), and was later home to the Kembery family. It was demolished in the 1960s.

Speedwell Road. This example of an eighteenth-century stone-walled cottage was situated next to the Speedwell Pit. In the 1940s it was used as an annex by the University Settlement. It was demolished in 1952 to make way for the Speedwell fire station.

Rock Cottage, which once stood on the hillside in Crews Hole. Originally owned by the Jones family, it was sold at public auction at the Don Johns pub in 1911 for £29. It was owned by the Hodge family until it was demolished in 1933. The photograph shows Edward Hodge, his wife Violet and sons Albert and Frank. Edward was probably a market gardener.

The Ship Inn, Clouds Hill Road/Bell Hill Road. Shown on the 1845 Tithe Map, by 1900 it had been substantially rebuilt and given the evocative name: the 'Worlds End'. A rank of large Victorian houses was built to the right of the adjacent lane which became Whiteway Road.

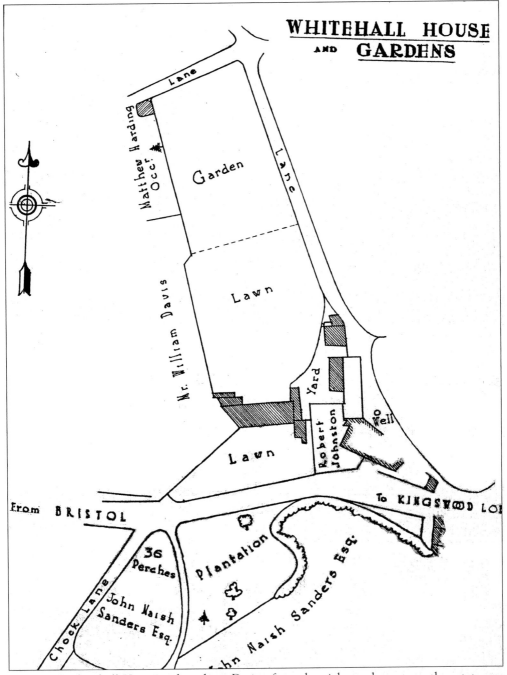

WHITEHALL HOUSE
AND GARDENS

Lane

Matthew Harding Occr.

Garden

Lane

Mr. William Davis

Lawn

Lawn

Yard

Robert Johnston

Well

From BRISTOL

To KINGSWOOD LO[...]

36 Perches

Chock Lane

John Naish Sanders Esq.

Plantation

John Naish Sanders Esq.

A plan of Whitehall House and gardens. Dating from the eighteenth century, the estate was owned by the Davis family. In the 1830s the house became a lunatic asylum, known locally as the Madhouse. The remains of the old house were removed for the construction of Whitehall school in 1879-1880.

Plummers Hill. This picture was taken from Speedwell Road, looking up Plummers Hill. Today houses line the left-hand side. On the right, prefabs replaced the former market gardens after 1945. The right-hand side used to flood on a regular basis.

Clouds Hill House. Born in Bedminster in 1872, Edwin Foss became a well respected Bristol physician and surgeon who lived at Summerhill House and later Clouds Hill House. After he died in 1935 the surgery at Clouds Hill House was carried on by his son Dr George Foss and daughter Dr Joan Foss. The surgery continued until 1970.

Two
The Park

In 1890, just weeks before his death, the local MP Handel Cossham stated his view that the area of St George should be provided with a public park. With its population rapidly growing, he stated that open spaces were swiftly disappearing. Cossham's ideas for the new park were advanced. He advocated the novel idea of including a stretch of artificial water, rightly seeing this as a radical departure for parks in the Bristol area. Although Cossham did not live to see it, the following twenty years did see the gradual evolution of a brilliantly designed park in St George.

Cossham indicated that land near his Holly Lodge House would be ideal for the new park, and that he would present this to the parish. However, after his death this suggestion was lost and the St George Board opted for a more central location.

In March 1894 the St George Local Board purchased, from the Ecclesiastical Commissioners, thirty-eight acres of land. The site centred on fields and a farmhouse known as the Fire Engine Farm. The area stretched north from the Fire Engine tavern to the Whitehall colliery and Rose Green and east to the old poorhouse. The Wainbrook flowed across the middle of the site with a footbridge across it. A number of paths cut across this land but there were few, if any, trees to form a basis for the park. To transform this area into a showcase for St George, the local board looked to one of its own to make the plans.

The surveyor of the St George Local Board, T. Lawrence Lewis produced a design remarkable for its stylish, co-ordinated and imaginative approach. In this he seemed to reflect Cossham's views of creating an area more 'park-like' and sophisticated than any of Bristol's urban parks. The plan was full of interesting and advanced touches. Its centrepiece was an elegant, ornamental lake which, unlike Eastville's, was not an afterthought but was vital to the overall design. Instead of random, haphazard paths, St George Park was designed to have axial paths with a classic focal point of a raised circular area with a bandstand in the middle. Around the lake was a well-executed serpentine walk. The main Church Road gateway was suitably impressive. In addition to all this was the exquisite Victoria Free Library, built in the south east corner. The overall impression was of a sharply focussed and radical design, a striking advert for St George.

Although opened in 1894, the grand plan was far from complete when Bristol took control from St George Board in 1897. Problems with water retention in the lake cast doubt on the bold scheme while the City surveyor reported that out of 450 newly planted trees, only 100 were alive. However, with a £7,000 cash injection, the basics of a fine park were in place. In true Edwardian fashion the additional 'features' were added. Elaborate drinking fountains and urinals were already in place. In 1905 a redundant naval gun was put on display and three years later tennis courts and a bowling green were added. Boating on the lake was to be a memorable activity for many years.

The Second World War and modern post war ideas had a considerable impact on the Park, and many of the fine details were lost. However despite all the changes, the Park has always been a much loved asset for the people of east Bristol. Throughout the years it has been a source of cherished and everlasting memories for its patrons.

The central bandstand area which was the focal point of the Park, seen here in the 1900s. The neat, surrounding hedges were removed in the 1970s. The site of the famous giant-draughts board was off left.

The lake, looking east towards the former poorhouse/pottery buildings. In 1941, nine acres of the park, near the lake, were dug up for allotments to aid the War effort.

The naval gun which stood in the centre of the triangle plot, near the Church Road entrance. Presented to Bristol Corporation by the Admiralty, this was one of three guns from HMS *Daedalus*. It was an 1860s 7-inch muzzle-loading-rifle (MLR) on an iron slide carriage. It should not be confused with captured Russian guns from the Crimean War! The naval gun was a popular feature of the Park until it was removed around 1941; its fate is unknown.

Drinking fountains were an important feature of Victorian parks, always popular with thirsty kids. The ornate and elaborate iron fountains were removed around 1941 for the war effort and replaced after the war by 'drinking stems'. These were regrettably removed during the 1970s.

Edwardian tranquility by the lake at St George Park. The lake, the 'jewel in the crown' of the Park, was completed between 1895 and 1897. Note the mobile boating hut; boating was regrettably withdrawn in 1993, the end of an era.

The playground, boating hut and lake at St George Park. This view was on a postcard sent on 10 June 1966.

One of the four piers at the main entrance to the Park. The gates were removed during the Second World War. The inscription commemorates Joseph Stubbs, clerk of the St George Board. The adjacent pier collapsed in 1979 and was not rebuilt.

A delightful Edwardian shot of the park. The tower of St George Church and the rear of the library stand out in the background. The area to the left later became the site of various types of play equipment.

Many will recall boating on the lake on a fine summer's afternoon and the various types of boats which could be hired from the green hut (demolished 1994).

The main gateway of St George Park and St George School. This is a classic early shot, showing St George Council's two major achievements. Note the smithy, which was replaced in 1938 by a new public toilet. The adjoining farriers cottages was also demolished.

26

In 1904 bylaws for pleasure grounds were clarified. The main rules were publicly displayed on notice boards in the park. Note that the park opened 8a.m. to 5.30p.m. in the winter. Summer hours were 7a.m. to 10p.m. These were the days of park keepers, gates and railings! St George Park also became a popular venue for holding political meetings in the Bristol East constituency.

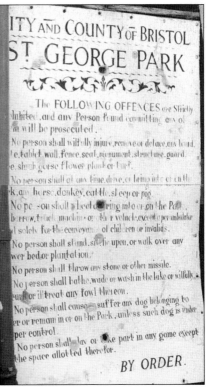

ITY AND COUNTY OF BRISTOL

ST. GEORGE PARK

The FOLLOWING OFFENCES are Strictly Inhibited, and any Person found committing any of them will be prosecuted.

No person shall wilfully injure, remove or deface any board, notice, tablet, wall, fence, seat, monument, structure, guard, tree, shrub, gorse, flower, plant or turf.

No person shall at any time, drive, or bring into or on the Park, any horse, donkey, cattle, sheep or pig.

No person shall wheel or bring into or on the Park, any barrow, truck, machine or other vehicle, except a perambulator used solely for the conveyance of children or invalids.

No person shall stand, sit, lie upon, or walk over any flower bed or plantation.

No person shall throw any stone or other missile.

No person shall bathe, wade or wash in the lake or wilfully disturb or ill treat any fowl thereon.

No person shall cause or suffer any dog belonging to him or her or remain in or on the Park, unless such dog is under proper control.

No person shall play or take part in any game except in the space allotted therefor.

BY ORDER.

Band Stand, The Park, St. George, Bristol

The bandstand: a classic park feature, surprisingly removed in 1958. Bands were an important and popular feature of the life of the park, from its very earliest days. The bandstand was also used as an open-air school.

St George Library or the Victoria Free Library as it was known when built in 1896. It was a gift from Sir William Henry Wills, the tobacco benefactor and MP for Bristol East from 1895 to 1900. This acclaimed architectural masterpiece was demolished in 1962 in preference for a design which could not have been more different.

New St George Library which was opened on 22 November 1963. It is visually dominated by vast panes of glass (lower ones later removed). Note that the boundary piers (with ball finials), walls and railings were retained from the original structure.

Three
Working Days

From coal mining to corsets the area boasted a rich and surprising variety of industry. Two examples were the Whitehall bakery and the manufacture of boots and shoes.

The Co-op Whitehall Bakery opened on 10 March 1910. It was situated between Chester Road and Howard Street. The site covered 5,813 sq yds, and it including stalls for thirty horses. By 1939 there were 100 bread rounds operating from here. There was a smaller bakery in Johnsons Road, Whitehall. This made cakes and buns. By 1961 because of competition, all bread was transferred to Whitby Road. The large site closed in 1969. Part if the building was later used by the police traffic section. It was all finally demolished in 1997 for housing.

Boots: Cheap mass-produced boots and shoes brought a lot of employment to St George and Kingswood. In 1881 there were at least five wholesale boot manufacturers in St Goerge. By 1916 that figure had risen to sixteen. That number was to decline in the 1930s/'40s and by the 1960s there were none left in St George. In the 1880s Bryant and Son set up a factory in Beaconsfield Road. The owner of the works lived next to the factory until they built their own house in Beaufort Road. This was known as 'The Poplar' and was later owned by the Ashmead family. Bryant's boot factory suddenly closed in the 1940s. Local children got in soon afterwards and found it just as Bryants had left it, as if it was ready for the next day's work.

Peckett's locomotive works, William Butler's tar works and Strachan & Henshaw were other local firms that gave employment to local people. They also gained renowned reputations.

'Very difficult working conditions' – the Speedwell Pit. Its origins went back to the eighteenth century and it finally closed in 1936.

Whitehall Bakery exterior. The scale of the building is clearly evident from this drawing. Chester Road is on the left, the road in the foreground is Park Crescent.

The busy ovens inside Whitehall Bakery.

A representation of the 'Fire Engine' at St George. Mining significantly benefited from the invention of the steam engine. Primarily used for pumping water out of pits, a Newcomen steam or 'fire engine' was used in the Whitehall area in the mid-eighteenth century. It gave its name to the Fire Engine Farm, the Fire Engine turnpike toll-house and the still surviving Fire Engine Inn.

Deep Pit was at the centre of a busy and harsh industrial landscape. In addition to the collieries (with their vast slag heaps), the area included quarries, Peckett's loco works and a mass of industrial railway lines. Interspersed were ranks of miners cottages, forming a close knit community. Both Deep Pit and Speedwell Pit closed in 1936.

Troopers Hill chimney, truly a Bristol landmark. On the very summit of the hill, it was part of a flue system associated with the eighteenth-century Crews Hole copper works. Troopers Hill has a dramatic appearance, a result of industrial use going back to medieval times when sandstone was quarried. Mining for coal, fire clay and iron ore all took place in and around the hill. Crews Hole, at the bottom of the hill, was an early area of intensive industrial activity. In a 1610 map of the Kingswood area, the area is called 'Harris Hill'.

Butler's Tar Distilling Works. Originally Roberts & Daines tar works, it was one of the earliest built in the country. William Butler was manager from 1843 before taking over ownership in 1863. He and his sons built up a very successful company on the banks of the Avon at Crews Hole. (Also see p. 98)

Crews Hole, a square two-stage chimney near Butler's Tar Works, at the bottom of Troopers Hill. A relic from colliery days, it would originally have been attached to an engine house.

Bryant's boot workers outside the tramway refreshment rooms, now the Fountain Café, on the corner of Church Road and Beaconsfield Road. On the opposite corner is the Labour Party's Walter Baker Hall. (see p.100)

Bryant's boot works, Beaconsfield Road. The road was named after Conservative Prime Minister Benjamin Disraeli, 1st Earl of Beaconsfield (1804-1881).

Woodingtons Boot Factory. Boot making was a cottage industry until the invention of machines which mechanized the process. From the 1870s small factories grew up in the St George and Kingswood areas, equipped with machines to manufacture boots. J.H. Woodington's factory was situated in Hillside Road at the junction with Kenn Road; a private health centre is now built on the site.

The Atlas loco works was located in Foundry Lane, very near to the Deep Pit. Originally Fox Walker & Co. of 1864 it was later taken over by Thomas Peckett. The works had an iron foundry, a boiler shop, carpentry and erecting shops plus a copper smiths brass foundry. The manufacture of various types of saddle tank engines was carried out until 1958, with the works closing in the 1960s.

Strachan & Henshaw, Ltd: originating in 1879, the Whitehall ironworks opened in 1904. Adjacent to the Whitehall Colliery, it bordered Church Lane. The main entrance was on Chalks Road, which led to a large yard with a gantry. The Whitehall works were demolished in June 1980 and new industrial units built.

A group of women workers at Strachan & Henshaw, probably during the First World War. In the 1960s the firm was known for producing printing and packaging machinery.

The workroom at Chappell Allen's corset works in the 1930s decorated for a celebration, perhaps the coronation of George VI in 1937. The works were located on the corner of Avonvale Road and Victoria Avenue.

Chappell Allen's corset works. The firm of Chappell, C.W. Allen & Co. was originally located in Weare Street, Bristol. By 1900 they were firmly established in Redfield as the Patriotic Corset Works. Many women were employed making undergarments. The ground floor contained the boiler room, offices and warehouse. In the 1930s the upper floors had two large rooms with about twenty or thirty long tables supporting the sewing machines. This landmark building, known as the 'stay factory', was demolished in August 1983.

Looking up Carlton Park. By 1903 Bristol Co-operative Society had constructed a Cabinet Works between Carlton Park and Gerrish Avenue. The building suffered severe fire damage during the Second World War when it was set alight by incendiary bombs, although by that time it was the Upholstery and Bedding Works of the Co-operative Wholesale Society Ltd.

Looking up Gerrish Avenue. The Co-op factory ran practically the full length of Gerrish Avenue. The centre of the building is where the offices were located. In the 1960s the factory was sold to B Maggs and Company of Queens Road, Clifton, the large department store. Furniture and beds continued to be made at Whitehall until early 1980 when the factory was closed. The buildings were demolished in August 1980 and Whitehall Trading Estate was built on the site.

Four

The Golden Miles

Memories of Church Road

On the corner of Dove Lane was the Dove public house. Just along were St Matthew's School rooms; these were pulled down in the 1950s and replaced by a pleasant little garden. On the other side of Church Road, between Heber Street and the Co-op, was a row of cottages with very pretty gardens – a little bit of country side left in the urban development. Continuing up the Road was Pople's newsagent near M. Ferris, the butcher. On the corner of Edward Street was a greengrocer, which has since been a hairdressers and is now a Chinese chippy. Then you had Mr Way's butchers shop, Martins sweetshop, Lewis china and a boot repairer next to the Albert Inn.

Back across the Road, adjoining St Matthews was the doctor's house. Doctor Alexander Houghton and later Dr Moore used this large house. Medical practice is of course now carried out in modern health centres, a far cry from Dr Alexander cycling around the district making his calls.

On the other corner of Bryon Street was a toy shop, then Miss White the haberdashers next to Mr Walker's cooked meat shop. In the rooms above him the local Labour Party used to hold their ward meetings, with entrance being obtained from Byron Street.

The Wine Shop on the corner of Morse Road, had been a temporary vicarage for Dr Stockwood in the 1940s. The Drs Struthers lived in 'Hillside' a relatively large house built in 1893. This was just up from Rees barbers and opposite the White Lion pub. The night bell can still be seen on the front porch. On the very next corner births and deaths could be registered. Between Witchell Road and Verrier Road was a milk bottling plant and a grocery warehouse. On the corner of Verrier Road was the Westminster Bank, followed by Andrews green grocers, a dry cleaners and then Mrs Stawte, a popular sweet and tobacconist. This was next to the Redfield post office on the corner of Weight Road. Although long gone, the pillar box still stands on the pavement. Past the National Provincial Bank you came to Willways laundry.

Across the Road from the Westminster Bank was a greengrocer (now a fried chicken outlet), Cuffs hairdresser and Lampards pastry parlour, wedding cakes a speciality. Past Hamilton Terrace was Hudds the pawnbroker and shop, reached by going up steps. Next to this was John James tv and radio. On the opposite corner of Victoria Parade was Gwilliams. Long queues would form here to buy his popular ham and cheese. A hardware store, Olivers shoes and the Granada brought you to Iven's the drapers. This was an interesting shop, you went in one door and came out of the other. It also had fine polished counters. Kifts furnishers (transformed in 1978 to NatWest), Pearks grocers, Carwardine coffee sellers, David Greigs (large grocers) and Hodders the chemist, brought you to Lyppiatt Road. On the other side of the Road, notable shops were Bressingtons fruit and veg, Haywards cash chemist and Mr Pearce the fishmonger. Pearce's shop had a marble angled slab, always full with different types of fish.

In the early 1960s Pearks built a supermarket on the corner of Roseberry Park. It changed its name to Maypole and finally to Liptons before closing. Next door Tesco opened their supermarket which was a big event for the area. These two modern structures replaced a Victorian rank which included Palmer's meat shop, a Co-op hardware store and a ladies dress shop.

Further up the Road next to Elkins the jewellers was a sweet shop. This was a popular place to stock up on confectionery before your walk around the park!

Joyce Peters and Dorothy Jones, 1987

Church Road in the 1920s with Salem Church on the right with the spire, (later removed). The church is on the corner of Salisbury Street, named after the Conservative Prime Minister of the 1890s, Lord Salisbury.

Redfield Inn, Church Road, on the corner of Brook Street. Dating from the 1870s, this pub survives although most of the houses in Brook Street were demolished in the 1960s. The landlord in 1944 was Mrs Rose Tambling.

Bikes, vans, cars and a tram in Church Road, August 1939. Witchell Road is off to the right. The White Lion, off left, (now the Old Stillage), survives today. Before 1899, a high wall on the right concealed Redfield House and its gardens.

Church Road, Redfield, August 1962. Kath Nurse (*née* Rees) is seen on the bike. In the background can be seen the White Lion pub, Williams television shop and the launderette. Behind the camera is John Rees barbers shop.

Bargains Galore – some unique shops still survive in Redfield and St George. Every day the owner of this shop, Ray Morgan, puts this display outside of his shop, 84 Church Road. It is a real 'Aladdins Cave' with traditional customer service. Ray took over in 1969, what had been Reg Walker's cooked meat shop.

Albert Inn, Church Road. Dating from the 1870s this corner shop off-licence is still situated on the corner of Albert Street. The houses in Albert Street were pulled down between 1967 and 1974.

Gwilliams: a fascinating and fondly remembered Redfield shop, full of character. Many residents of the area will recall queuing for its superb ham. The building, on the corner of Victoria Parade, was built in 1873 and was called Victoria House. Its old-fashioned charm remained until it was finally demolished in January 1982. Gwilliams traded from new premises in Church Road until 1998.

Moreton's

BRISTOL'S HIGH-CLASS BUTCHERS

at your Service

—★—

from

★

1919

Branches at :

Whiteladies Road,
Westbury-on-Trym,
Cotham,
Redfield.

Moretons, Church Road, a popular butcher's shop next to the Granada. In the 1980's it became Heals although traditional style (including sawdust on the floor) remained. It closed in 1998, the building being incorporated in to J.D. Wetherspoons pub 'St Georges Hall'. Moretons became the site of the pub's main entrance.

Church Road in the 1920s: a shot from Victoria Parade to the old Redfield Methodist Sunday School room. Built in the 1840s, it was used by the church until 1884; it has since been occupied by the St George Liberal Club. It is one of Church Road's oldest surviving structures.

This rank of shops on Church Road included a sweet shop on the corner of Worsley Street (off left). This shop had a lending library at the back (like Martins further down) and also sold some toys. Its neighbours were Haywards cash chemists, Hudds opticians, Pearces fishmongers and the still surviving newsagents. Worsley Street was named after P.J. Worsley who was the director of the Netham Chemical Works.

Tesco on Church Road is a Redfield landmark and a symbol of the new, modern 1960s when it was opened by 'Coco the Clown'. Originally two separate stores, 'Home & Wear' and grocery, it is the oldest surviving Tesco in Bristol but is continually updated. Green Shields Stamps were a big feature of the store's early days. One of the book's authors, David Cheesley relates his memories of the grand opening, on 22 August 1967, for the recent St George video produced by First Take.

The interior of Pearks on Church Road. Like Maypole and David Greig, Pearks were traditional grocers who occupied 221 Church Road from 1921. Doreen Parsons and colleagues can be seen serving in pre-supermarket days.

The Rising Sun on Church Road, next to the Black Horse and opposite the Horse & Jockey. This interesting Redfield pub closed in the late 1960s, becoming a store for nearby Taylor's builders merchants. The building was demolished in 1983, although the site was redeveloped eleven years later with a new structure for William Hill's the bookmakers.

The Horse and Jockey, Church Road, another local pub no longer with us. It was demolished in 1997 to make way for the new Aldi Supermarket. In 1944 the pub was named the Old Horse and Jockey and the landlord was William Preston.

The George and Dragon, Church Road. To local people this pub is always referred to as 'Monty's' – the reason being that the landlord in 1944 and for many years was Montague Janes. To the side of the pub is George and Dragon Lane which at one time lead through to Pile Marsh. It is now overgrown and blocked up.

Fire Engine Inn on the corner of Church Road and Blackswarth Road. The pub name has nothing to do with fire fighting but is named after the primitive steam engine used at the nearby coal pit by its owner John Armitstead, from around 1800. Directly facing the pub was Fire Engine Farm which later became St George Park. The landlord in 1944 was Henry Robbins. The pub dates from around 1769.

A view of Church Road in April 1939, looking towards Salem Church. The first two houses on the left were demolished in the 1970s. A petrol station replaced the buildings on the corner of Seneca Street (off right). Lafferty's sweet and tobacconist shop (extreme right) is on the corner of a footpath called the Wicket, which leads to Blackswarth Road, via Cossham Road.

Opened in 1947 Mark Deacon, Church Road, was one of Bristol's oldest menswear shops. The shop was initially owned by the late Mark Deacon and his wife Hilda, although they were joined in 1951 by Donald Speirs, who in recent years ran the shop with his son Mark. It closed in May 2001.

In 1910 James 'Jimmy' Hodges set up his hairdressing and barbers shop at 324 Church Road. The same business survives today, ran by his son Brian. During the War a bomb dropped opposite the shop on the edge of St George Park. This nearly closed the shop down, as did the fashion for very long hair in the 1960s!

Brian Hodges inside his traditional barbers shop. He took over from his father in 1953.

The public drinking fountain and water trough for horses at the junction of the Kingswood and Hanham roads. The memorial stone was laid by William Butler. On the left behind the trees is Clouds Hill House, the home of the Foss family. This view was printed on a postcard sent on 15 September 1963.

Bristol Omnibus FLF double decker heads for Kingswood, along Clouds Hill Road on Route 88 in the late 1960s when Bristol buses were green and cream. A Silver MK2 Ford Cortina follows behind.

Taylor's shop: Edward George Taylor and Sons established this small grocer's shop at 5 Clouds Hill Road, before the Second World War. Typical of hundreds of similar looking small shops in east Bristol, it managed to survive where others didn't after the opening of Tesco, Co-op and other supermarkets. It finally closed in the late 1990s after over fifty years of service in St George.

Mr Sims, a local butcher, whose shop was at 3 Clouds Hill Road.

The Prince of Wales public house at No. 88 Clouds Hill Road. On the corner of Bethel Road, this pub was de-licensed and demolished in the 1970s. The site is still empty.

Left: The Co-op, Clouds Hill Road, between the World End and Bethel Methodist Church. It opened in 1904 and closed in the 1980s. A group of ex-employees ran it for a while. *Right:* Church Road, Redfield, 1937. John Rees and his son Edward, stand proudly outside No. 96. John cut hair at this location for forty years. To the right was a wine shop and then Morse Road.

Electric Spark, Clouds Hill Road. Dating from the late 1930s, this classic ironmongers is still going strong.

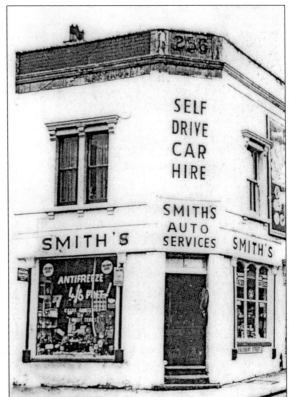

Ken Smiths, Church Road. This opened in 1958; it had previously been Millards car accessories. Ken is well known for his very impressive Christmas light display which he puts up every year to raise money for charity.

William Gray's fishmongers and greengrocers, No. 35 Bell Hill Road, in between the Worlds End and Battenburg Road. Gray's served the community for over fifty years.

The Bell Hotel at St George: a large pub on Bell Hill Road, which was popular for wedding receptions. For a while in the 1980s it was called the 'Thomas Usher', before reverting to its historic name.

54

Church Road has always been called The Road by locals. It has been home, over the years, to a varied and rich selection of shops and businesses. This advertising card gives a flavour of Church Road in the 1920s. Note the prominant promotion of St Matthew's Moorfields.

The Air Balloon Tavern on Air Balloon Road. This pub was built by George's Brewery in the early 1900s on the site of a previous pub called the Crown and Anchor. The name Air Balloon Tavern was chosen to commemorate the landing of a hot air balloon on nearby Troopers Hill which must have been a very important local event. The landlord in 1944 was Frank Osborne, the maternal grandfather of David Cheesley one of this book's authors.

The Osborne family in the back garden of the Air Balloon Tavern around 1946. Left to right: Jean, mother Mary Ann and father Frank.

An Edwardian view looking up Nags Head Hill. Off to the left is the very steep Stibbs Hill and off to the right is Troopers Hill Road. The Lord Raglan pub still survives and new houses were built on the right after the First World War. The landlord in 1944 was Albert Bateman.

Tram 172 on Clouds Hill Road. Plummers Hill is on the left. Further on are the railings of Summerhill School, the Baptist Church and the buildings that were demolished for the modern school extension. Further up on the right, was an old public house called the Cherry Orchard.

An early rank of smaller dwellings and shops on Church Road opposite St George School.

Kath Rees on the junction of Morse Road and Church Road in the 1950s. On the corner of Edward Street is the Regent fruiterer and florist. Next door is Ferris' butchers shop. The house with the bike outside belonged to Harry Jones, a longstanding Redfield character. Poples newsagent and Miss Chriscilla Evans decorating shop can also be seen.

White Hart on Whitehall Road, a large stone-built pub with large garden adjoining, which has now become a car park. The landlord in 1944 was Walter Clements. In the 1960s and '70s the landlord was Anthony Gallipolli Crotty, a real local character. His speciality every Saturday night at closing time was to sing *My Brother Sylvest*, much to the amusement of the locals.

The Red Lion, a typical Victorian corner pub, on the corner of Whitehall Road and Lyppiatt Road. The landlord in 1944 was Henry Britton. Lyppiatt Road, formerly Lyppiatt Lane, is one of the oldest roads in the district.

Morris' sweet shop on Whitehall Road. Many Whitehall School kids will recall this popular and distinctive 'tuck shop' on the corner of Woodbine Road. It was known as 'Monkey Morris', because of a caged monkey in the shop.

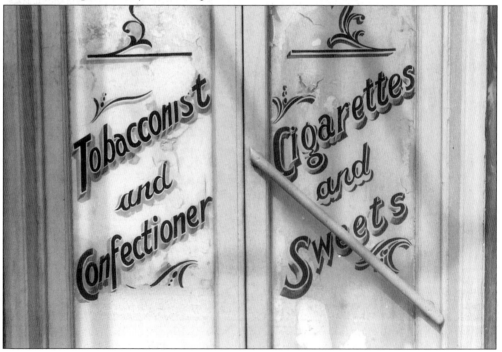

The 1900s grocery store, the Co-op, No. 290 Whitehall Road: a butchers section was added later. Like neighbouring Co-ops, it was remembered for its precisely cut blocks of cheese and butter. Biscuits, tea and sugar were also measured to your requirements. The building survives but the Co-op has long gone.

The Kings Head on the Corner Whitehall Road and Gordon Road. The Maggs and Parsons families owned this pub for many years. Within living memory, this property was surrounded by extensive outbuildings, including stables and a dairy. It also had an orchard and paddock. The present car park has been built on the site of the pub's former garden.

Brains drapers, 113 Bell Hill Road. The Brains served the community from around 1910 to around 1940. This shop was situated opposite the Bell public house.

Outside John (Jack) Rees hairdressers, No. 96 Church Road. Just around from Morse Road, John cut hair from the 1930s to 1978. The name of the girl is unknown.

Five

Chapels and Churches

The creation of St George Church was an important milestone in the history of the area, indeed giving its name to the district. The nineteenth century saw the strong growth of methodism which was to have a profound impact on the area. One Methodist chapel which emerged was Bethesda.

Bethesda Methodist Church, Redfield: In December 1999, Bethesda Methodist Church vacated the building which had been used for its worship for 130 years. The church moved a short distance across Avonvale Road, to its Sunday School building. Plans are in place to modernize the school building to create a modern place for worship in the twenty-first century.

The origins of Bethesda go back to the 1850s and a group of Methodists who met in a chapel in Two Mill Hill, St George. In 1852 they opened a New Wesleyan chapel in Lyppiatt's Lane, Redfield. The subsequent success and growth of the chapel was considerably helped by the support of influential backers. Among these were Mr Worsley, director of Netham Chemical Works and William Butler, the tar manufacturer. A key benefactor and supporter was William Stone, a successful hay and straw dealer. He later lived with his wife, Anne, in Redfield's grandest residence, the Redfield House estate. In 1868, Stone conveyed to William Butler and nineteen other trustees a plot of land in Redfield for new, larger church premises. This piece of land was known as Lyppiatt's Leaze. It was described as fronting the turnpike road to Bristol (Church Road). This land was also adjacent to the George and Dragon public house and contained a well (from which the name Bethesda was derived).

The new Bethesda Methodist Church was opened on 18 August 1869. Twelve years later William Stone provided land from the Redfield House estate, for the building of a Sunday School. A major donor again was William Butler but others included Messrs Fry and Son and Messrs Sparke Evans & Co. The Sunday School opened in April 1883.

St George Parish Church: In the long hot summer of 1976, St George Church was demolished. As the parish church, its history and tradition was deeply ingrained in the story of the area. There were three churches in the same site, the last, built in 1880, was a very impressive structure. The lofty elaborate tower with spirelet was a local landmark. Overall the quality of the building and its importance to the history of the area gave St George Church a real significance. Its visual presence was heightened by a prominent physical location and extensive surrounding land. To the west was the church school for boys (later the parish hall). The girls' school was opposite the church adjoining Post Office Lane. On the south side was the large graveyard. To the east was a substantial vicarage. One of its occupants was the Revd George Henry Willmott Elwell who was vicar for over forty-five years until the late 1960s.

A selection of churchs and chapels, some now closed but some very much still active, are included in this chapter.

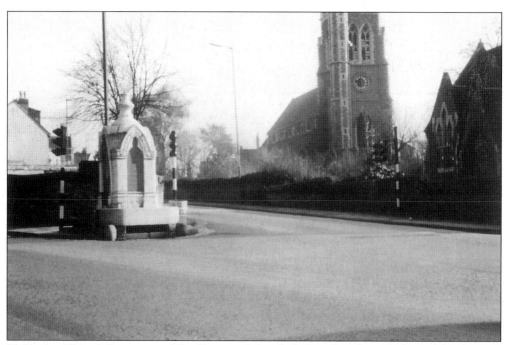

St George Church looms over 'The Fountain' shortly before demolition. The portland stone, gothic style drinking fountain was an 1896 gift from William Butler. The traffic lights were installed in 1963.

A rare interior shot of St George Church; demolition was imminent.

St George Church from the south. The rambling and impressive vicarage was to the right, bordering Harvey's Lane. The second church was destroyed by fire in 1878 and replaced by this imposing building. Revd John Emra was vicar from 1809-1842. He was described as a conscientious parson in a poor, large and scattered parish.

The demolition of St George Church. The church had a tower, spire and six bells. Demolition of the church commenced on 25 July 1976. In this view, demolition is nearly complete, only the spire remains. It was razed to the ground and replaced by modern flats for the elderly.

Bethesda Methodist Church, Redfield, opened 1869. To the left is Bethesda Villa. This later became the Minister's house. To the right is Avonvale Road originally called George Lane.

The interior of Bethesda, looking towards Church Road. This building was last used for worship in December 1999.

Bethesda Sunday School's Whitsun parade in the 1960s. This is Church Road with the Rising Sun and Black Horse in the background. Whitsun was an important occasion for Methodists. The Whitsuntide procession saw Methodists and other denominations in East Bristol, parade through the streets.

Bethesda centenary party, October 1969, in the Sunday School room which had been built in 1883.

The wedding of Susan Jones and Richard Davis at St Matthew in 1968. In the background is the large Masons Arms off licence, demolished in the mid-1970s. The wedding party are standing in Cowper Street which dates from the 1880s. It was probably named after Lord Cowper, a member of Gladstone's Liberal Government.

St Matthew Moorfields, which opened in 1873 and closed in 1998. This church had a high profile when Mervyn Stockwood was vicar, between 1941 and 1955. St Matthew's was instrumental in the creation of the Redfield United Front. The RUF comprised of eight local churches, co-operating socially and in the spreading of the gospel.

Clowes Methodist Church on Air Balloon Road was built in 1879 with seating for 400. The building was demolished in 1989 and a new church erected, which was set back from the road. Bristol East Band was associated with Clowes for many years.

St Michael's, Two Mile Hill. Opened in 1848, it consists of a chancel, nave and north aisle. It was seen as a smaller version of St George Church and was of an advanced design for its date, in the gothic revival style.

Bethel United Methodist Church, dating from 1858 and situated on Clouds Hill Road. It closed around 1987, although the much-changed building is still in existence as a fitness centre.

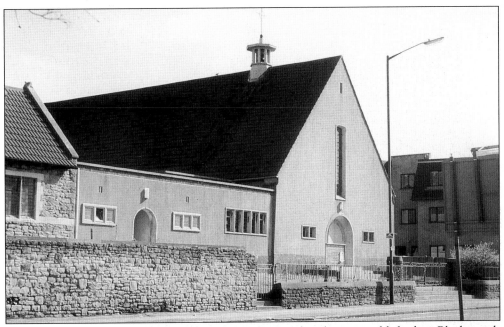

St Leonard's Church, Redfield: A temporary mission church was established in Blackswarth Road in 1908 and the present church was built in 1938, an award winning design in its day.

St Patrick's RC Church which was founded by Father William Dillon and opened in 1923. A new church building and complex, built on Grindell's field, was completed in 1995.

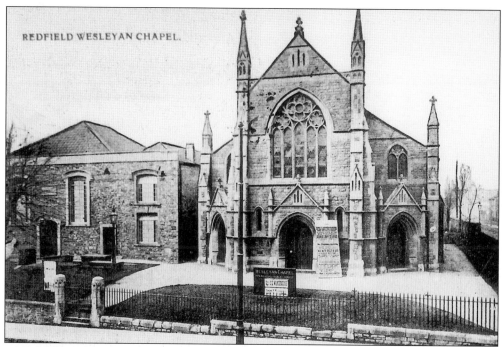

Redfield Methodist Chapel was opened in 1884 and took the place of the 1815 Redfield Chapel which became the Sunday School building. The new chapel was built on the site of the minister's old house and garden. Joined with Bethesda from 1965, it closed ten years later. The building has been used as a Hindu temple since 1981.

An interior view of Redfield Methodist Chapel. Redfield's Revd Ronald Spivey, together with Mervyn Stockwood, were the prime movers behind the creation of the Redfield United Front.

A close up of the pulpit at Redfield Methodist.

Reg Gregory (centre) assembling the 36th Boys Brigade to lead the Redfield United Front fancy dress procession, Whit Monday 1951. This view is Gilbert Road, note the bus stop.

Salem Methodist Chapel. This chapel was built to an elegant design in the early gothic style and opened 13 January 1904. It replaced the 'cow shed' above the mission room on the same site. Now in use as Bethel United Church, it was also the base of the 38th Boys Brigade Company.

St Ambrose: referred to as the 'cathedral of East Bristol' because of its grand scale. Consecrated in 1913, an adjacent mission church had first been established in 1905. It has an impressive three-stage tower. It is also the nearest church to Rose Green School.

Whitehall Zion Methodist Chapel: a 1907 structure on the corner of Neath Road. It replaced the original 1871 chapel which became the Sunday School and was later demolished to make way for a petrol station. Whitehall School pupils will remember services held in this adjacent church.

The imposing former vicarage of St Matthew Moorfields, on Whitehall Road. Vicarage Road is off to the left. The building has been used as a day nursery since the 1940s.

The large and elaborate vicarage of St George Church. Adjacent to Harvey's Lane, it was set in extensive grounds to the east of the church. It was demolished in 1976. For many years part of the base of Don John's Cross was situated in the vicarage gardens.

Six

Down Our Street

Delores Powell recalls memories of a special street in Redfield:

It is my privilege to write about Derby Street, a street in Redfield. It was a street I loved and in which I felt safe and secure. It was where all my grandparents and great-grandparents lived.
People used to say, 'No good ever came out of that street!' Perhaps I am biased but I know of so many people who truly loved, and still do, the soul of this street. Through all its poverty and suffering it was filled with so much that was good.
   Derby Street was filled with one large extended family. They had intermarried for years. They knew each other's background and history. They were the Helps, Hales, Hopes, Shepherds, Coles, Reas, Cooks, Leonards, Morgans, Vincents, Iles, Toogoods, Simmonds and Roberts. I could go on and on. I was known to all of them as 'Our Tom's Girl'.
   Although they were poor, they were scrupulously clean and had a natural dignity. If there were bare floorboards in their homes they were scrubbed as clean as the outside doorstep. They coveted little in terms of material possessions. The furniture they possessed only just met their basic needs. A scrubbed table, sturdy chairs and a couple of fireside rockers where they could sit, talk and relax. The men smoked their clay pipes and the women enjoyed their pinches of snuff. No television in those days, they were content to sit, look at and share time with each other.
   Although the houses of Derby Street are not longer there, the street itself remains. If only it could speak, what stories it would tell.
The Derby Street people certainly knew how to party. Pianos were pulled from homes on to the narrow strip of stone which still remains. People gathered around, they sang and danced. There were also brightly coloured piano accordions, mouth organs, drums, cymbals and tambourines and there were also those who could skilfully play the 'bones'. There were violins, too – yes, I can remember the violins!
   In case it might be thought I am looking at Derby Street through rose-coloured spectacles, I can only speak as I found. It was before I was born when Derby Street was known for its drunken brawls and fights. Passions evidently ran high and the low economic situations and ever-increasing families caused many a couple stress almost beyond endurance.
   To bring the story up-to-date, my dad's younger brother Gilbert Hale recently died. The illness with which he suffered caused him to wander. His family and the police were wonderful. They all knew where to find him. You guessed it! They would find him, more often than not, standing on the street where his roots were. The houses are no longer there but I doubt that that mattered to Gilbert. He knew, like me, that Derby Street's soul and roots would always remain.

The Steam Hammer, a beer retailer on the corner of Derby Street and Barnes Street. Derby Street, the houses in Barnes Street, nearby Shaftesbury Terrace and Stanley Street, were all demolished by 1972.

Delores Powell surveys the scene in Derby Street as it looks today. The houses of Derby Street were demolished between 1967 and 1970. However one house, No. 60 near Shaftesbury Terrace, remained standing derelict into the 1980s. The street was named after the 14th Earl of Derby who was Prime Minister in the 1850s and 1860s.

Susan Jones in Morse Road, Redfield in the 1950s. This view looks towards Edward Street and Way's butchers shop. Mr and Mrs Way traded until around 1975. Previously Albert Stirret, also a butcher, traded at the same location.

Later style terraced houses, distinguished from earlier examples by the larger bay windows, in Leonard Road, Redfield. These terraced houses were built on the grounds of the Redfield House estate.

Doreen Parsons (*née* Sheeley) outside her house in Victoria Avenue in the 1930s. This view looks towards Avonvale Road. The pram was a prized possession!

Mealings, a traditional corner shop on Victoria Avenue/Leonard Road. Many Redfield residents will recall using Mealings for shoe and boot repairs. In the 1990s the shop was converted into flats.

Alfred Parfitts grocery shop, Victoria Parade/Stephen Street. This traditional shop front survived until the late 1990s. After her husband died, Mrs Parfitt used the premises as a charity shop.

Children in fancy dress celebrate the Coronation in Morse Road in 1953. This Redfield road, dating from the mid-1880s, was named after Morse Goulter.

Morse Road residents celebrate the Coronation 1953, outside the appropriately named 'Jubilee Villa'. The group includes: Mrs Roberts, Mrs Robins, Mrs Burchill and Mrs Jones (extreme right).

The Coronation celebrations in Witchell Road, Redfield, in 1953. The Queen's Silver Jubilee party was held in the same road in 1977.

The Whitsun procession on Beaufort Road. Note that all are wearing hats!

The one remaining house on Edward Street, Redfield, now part of a motorcycle shop, formerly Bill Way's the butcher. Edward Street was one of the Redfield streets demolished in the 1960s. Others included Orchard Square, Albert Street and Clifton Street.

Avon Park, Redfield. The Furnivall family lived at No. 23, which backed onto Orchard Square. These shots date from the 1950s. Number 23 and its neighbouring houses were demolished, along with Orchard Square, to make way for elderly persons' flats. *Top left* is Les Furnivall with Avonvale Road in the distance. *Top right* is Brian Furnivall on his Triumph Tiger Cub.

Avon Battalion Boys' Brigade parade down Avonvale Road to the 36th Boys' Brigade HQ at Bethesda Church, on the occasion of the 50th anniversary.

The Cross and Anchor Hall, Gilbert Road. This fine hall was, until 1980, the HQ of the 36th Boys' Brigade. The 36th was founded in 1934 at the Redfield Methodist Church. The founding captain was Reg Gazzard. From 1969 to 1983, Reg Gregory (pictured here in 1934) was captain. He later became president of the 36th, which is now based at Bethesda Church.

An example of 1930s housing development near Troopers Hill.

Prefabs in Plummers Hill, St George. Bristol had over 3,000 houses totally destroyed during the Blitz. As war came to an end in 1945 factory built prefabricated bungalows were under construction. Many were erected in St George, like these at Plummers Hill. At the time their design was the most modern available featuring central heating, up-to-date kitchens, built-in cupboards and even a fridge.

Seven

The Happiest Days
of Our Lives

The growth in the number of elementary schools in the late nineteenth century reflected the increase in population. This against a background of significant education acts of Parliament in 1870 and 1902. New schools at Summerhill and Whitehall were early examples in the St George area. The Bristol School Board took control from St George in 1897 and added Redfield School and a new block at Summerhill. After 1902 responsibility passed to the Local Education Authority who built Air Balloon and Rose Green to the lastest designs. St Particks RC School and Speedwell both date from the 1930s. The St George School Board was particularly active and in a radical move created St George Higher Grade School.

St George School has existed since 1894 under various names and has survived many changes. In its first guise, St George Higher Grade and Technical School opened on 15 November 1894. Planned, built and run by the St George Local Board, it was, like St George Park, a pioneering, bold move by St George. The Board gained much of its revenue from so called 'whisky money'. This was a tax on beer and spirits given to the local councils in 1892. St George decided to plough the money into a school for technical and scientific education.

Fees were payable but a number of free placed were filled by competition. St George was the first of Bristol's Higher Grade Schools. The others, Merrywood and Fairfeld, were both opened after St George. By 1907 St George was fully established as a secondary grammar school, strictly split into boys and girls.

As well as elementary science, subjects taught included algebra, poetry, drawing, French and woodwork. The structure itself was compact in actual area, but imposing; adjacent to both Church Road and the Park, its height and red bricks made it a prominent landmark.

The school's reputation developed under Mr Pickles who was headmaster from 1896 to 1929. In 1957 Mr Discombe succeeded Dr Baldwin as head and led the school through the change to a comprehensive system.

The 1965 school, now called St George Comprehensive was a split site school formed around the grammar school together with Carlton Park Boys and Redfield Senior Girls School. The Second World War had halted talk of a new building at Whitehall, but in 1967 work started on new school buildings next to Carlton Park. The new Russell Town Avenue complex opened in 1970. However the old buildings at the Park, Victoria Avenue and Carlton Park remained in use. While all these changes were taking place, Mr Discombe fought a considerable battle with the authorities to retain the name 'St George School'. His success was a lasting achievement.

In 1975 Glyn Morgan took over as headmaster. By this time the Rose Green School buildings had also been added to St George Comprehensive, while a further new block at Russell Town Avenue replaced the old Redfield School. By the time the school's centenary was celebrated in 1994, it was wholly based in Russell Town Avenue. The original, fondly remembered red brick building closed in 1988.

Throughout all these changes the aim of giving pupils the best possible secondary education, whatever their background persisted. For many former pupils and staff, St George School left nothing but happy memories.

An architectural landmark: the building housing St George School from 1894 to 1988. It is now used as a community centre by the Bristol Indian Association.

A class pictured soon after the opening of St George Higher Grade School. Note the headmaster in the background.

Summerhill Infants' School. The pre-1884 school on the corner of Clouds Hill Road was opened by the St George School Board. The former Baptist Chapel building was later incorporated into the school.

Summerhill School, Plummers Hill. This adjacent block to the infants' was built in 1899 by Bristol School Board. Like the infants', the school is still serving the community.

Whitehall School which was opened in 1880 and built in the heavy Victorian gothic style of the time. Post-war pupils will remember the headmaster Mr Dixon and long serving Mr Stainer. The building was seen as obsolete by 1946 but was home to Whitehall Infants' until 1984. The juniors had vacated to new premises in 1976. Highly regarded by many former pupils and staff, the vast roofs and pointed windows finally came crashing down in 1986.

A group event at Whitehall School; looking towards Whitehall Road, c. 1972. The houses in the background (left) were demolished for the widening of the Chalks Road junction.

Miss Pugh, the headmistress of Whitehall Infants School, in the infants' hall with an early 1970s class. The group includes: Andy Jones, Gary Davis and David Ellis.

The rear entrance of Whitehall School on Bournville Road. The heavy, iron-gate led to the rear playground. The school had been built on the site of Whitehall House, a grand residence surrounded by extensive gardens (see p. 19). Modern houses now stand on the site.

Rose Green School on Whitehall Road which, in design terms, was a development of the style already seen with Redfield and Air Balloon. Opened in 1907 it was to have a complicated, if relatively short history. In the 1950s Rose Green was a girls' grammar school. At this time it was the only school in Bristol to provide both grammar school, academic and commercial courses. It was briefly part of Whitefield School in the 1960s, but the building finally became home to St George Rose Green Lower School, although closure came in 1984. The site was levelled to build houses two years later.

The rear of Rose Green School. The lower hall is on the right, and there were two further, hammer beam, central halls. The huts off to the left, were a relic of the East Bristol Central School, (1919-1941). Thurstons Barton was behind the camera.

Air Balloon Junior School with the infants' off to the right. Both date from 1905 and are still in use. Air Balloon School was built in the Art Nouveau style and was similar in layout to Redfield and Rose Green schools. It was built around hammer beam central halls with classrooms leading off on each side. A manual instruction centre and a cookery room were also part of the original design.

Recorder practice at Speedwell Girls School, 1960s. The Speedwell Senior Girls School opened in 1934, and was housed in a very neat and impressive building. Unfortunately it was destroyed by fire in 1974.

93

Susan Jones and friends at Redfield School in the 1950s.

The Avonvale Road side of Redfield School which was directly opposite Grindell's big house and stables. Just along the road was Capps, a fondly remembered sweet shop on the corner of Gladstone Street. It was the tuck shop of Redfield School!

94

Boys, girls and infants in a modern (by 1900 standards) 'central hall plan' at Redfield School. After 1945, this site became the base for Redfield Senior Girls School, although infants remained until the late 1950s. From 1965 it was part of St George Comprehensive. This complex, on the corner of Victoria Avenue and Avonvale Road, was converted into offices in 1975.

A group shot at Redfield School from the 1950s. The Redfield end of Victoria Avenue was originally called Queens Park. Victoria Square was the Barton Hill end. They were joined together as Victoria Avenue around 1905.

95

St Patrick's School, founded by Canon Dillon in 1933, an infant and primary school for many years. It was built on part of Grindell's Field. Grindell was a notable horse dealer who lived in a big house on the corner of Pilemarsh and Avonvale Road.

SCHOOL BOARD FOR ST. GEORGE

BRISTOL.

The New Schools on Barton Hill, known as the AVON VALE BOARD SCHOOLS, will be formally

OPENED AT A PUBLIC MEETING,

To be held on Saturday Afternoon, April 19, 1884

The Chair will be taken by the Rev. J. T Baylee, Chairman of the Board, at Four o'clock, and Messrs. W. H. Butler, H. Cossham, T. Parks, A. G. Verrier, and other Members of the Board are expected to be present.

Parents and Friends are invited to attend and inspect the Buildings and Playgrounds.

Scholars will be received on Monday morning, April 21st, at Nine o'clock, by the following head teachers:—

Boys' School   -   Mr. T. J. MacNamara.
Girls'   ,,   -   Miss E. Thompson.
Infants',,   -   Miss C. R. Horwood.

FREE.   per week.

Boys and Girls, Fourth Standard and above   **3**d.
    ,,   Below Standard four   -   **2**d.
Infants   .   .   .   -   **2**d.

(Signed)   **A. T. PHILPOTT,** clerk

Barton Hill was split between Bristol and St George councils. In 1884 Avonvale School was opened by St George. This notice from the time lists some of St George Board's most prominent figures, namely: W.H. Butler, Cossham, Verrier, Baylee and Philpott.

Eight
Famous Folk

A number of influential figures have had connections with the area over the years. Some prominent local businessmen, landowners and politicans are buried in the St George Cemetery at Avonview.
Avonview Cemetery: 6,231 acres of land at Beaufort Road became the cemetery of St George. Formerly known as Mugland Farm, it was purchased from W.J. Dix and W. Sealy in June 1881. The St George Board of Health opened the site in 1883.

There are many distinguished local people buried at Avonview. These include Handel Cossham MP and Albert Verrier. A successful tailor, Verrier was active in local issues from politics to sport. He was also chairman of the St George Board. Members of land-owning families such as the Hemmings, Fussells, Gerrished and Grindells are also buried at the cemetery. Imposing monuments mark the resting-place of William Butler and William Henry Butler both prominent figures in the history of the area.

Vast burial monuments in the original upper part of Avonview. The cemetery was extended twice and now stretches to Blackswarth Road.

William Butler was born in Leicestershire in 1819. He worked for the Bristol and Exeter Railway under Brunel, before coming to Bristol in 1843 to manage the Crews Hole tar distilling works. Butler acquired the ownership of the works in 1863.

His community activities were wide and influential. He was the prime mover behind the creation of the St George Local Board and was its chairman for fourteen years. He was chairman of the Highways Board, a magistrate and the first chairman of the Bristol Tramways and Carriage Company. Butler was closely connected with the Methodist Church and was a trustee of Bethesda Redfield. He retired in 1889 from active management of the tar works. He died eleven years later and was buried at Avonview on a site overlooking Crews Hole.

William Henry Butler, born 1850: eldest son of William Butler. He started work in the Crews Hole works in 1868, becoming Chairman in 1905. Like his father he was a member of the St George Local Board, a magistrate and an active supporter of the Methodist Church. He was Chairman of the Trustees who administered the estate of Handel Cossham, so enabling the building of Cossham Hospital. For many years he lived in Summerhill House, St George.

98

Handel Cossham, born in Thornbury in 1825. Cossham was a respected and popular local figure as well as a successful businessman with considerable interests in St George. He held strong religious views and his Non-conformist and political convictions deeply influenced how he ran his business interests.

In 1848 after studying mining, he went into partnership to extract coal in the Bristol area. By 1879 the successful business was under the sole ownership of Cossham. His mines included two in the parish of St George: Deep Pit and Speedwell.

He was keen to promote the welfare of his 1,500 employees and urged a conciliatory management style, rare in the harsh world of mining. Cossham was a champion of mass education and joined the Local Board. A staunch Liberal, in 1885 Cossham was elected as MP for Bristol East. He was firmly on the radical wing of the Liberal Party.

The grave and memorial of Handel Cossham, Avonview. Handel Cossham died unexpectedly in April 1890. In one of his last ever speeches, he stated that part of the pleasure of his life was to plan and lay out a public park for St George (see Chapter Two). His reputation was such that over 40,000 people watched his funeral procession as it made its way to Avonview cemetery St George. Cossham Hospital and Cossham Road were named in his honour.

A picture celebrating the preaching of John Wesley and George Whitefield. At Rose Green school a plaque was erected to mark the eighteenth-century open-air preaching of John Wesley and George Whitefield. A modernised version was reset on Whitehall Road when the school was demolished. A gifted speaker and organiser, Wesley prompted the growth of Methodism. The Methodist movement drew its main support from the 'common people' and became very strong in the St George and Kingswood areas.

WALTER JOHN BAKER, 1876—1930

Walter John Baker: The first Labour MP for Bristol East. A trade unionist (General Secretary of the Post Office Workers) and a member of the Fabian Society, Baker captured Bristol East by 2,036 votes in 1923. The 1923 general election marked an important advance by Labour into the remaining Liberal strongholds in the industrial cities. Baker's victory ended the area's long association with Liberal MPs. By the time of his death in 1930, Bristol East was an impregnable citadel for the Labour Party.

Stafford Cripps, was the British Ambassador to Moscow during the Second World War, a member of the War Cabinet, the Chancellor of the Exchequer (1947-1950), a brilliant lawyer and loyal churchman. Richard Stafford Cripps was elected MP for Bristol East in January 1931. It was such a Labour stronghold that he held on to it in the disaster that struck the Labour Party in the 1931 general election. In 1945 Cripps won Bristol East by almost 18,000 votes and Prime Minister Attlee made him President of the Board of Trade. He resigned from the Government in 1950, dying a year later.

In 1950 Tony Benn succeeded Stafford Cripps as Labour MP for Bristol South East. In the early 1960s he fought a personal battle to renounce his peerage and remain an MP. Many local supporters helped him in this campaign and the above notice dates from this period. In 1963 with victory eventually won, Benn addressed his supporters from the balcony of St George School, Church Road. Tony Benn remained Bristol South-East's high profile MP until 1983.

Dr Edwin Foss and friends enjoying a game of cricket on the lawn of Summerhill House in the early 1930s. For over fifty years in the nineteenth century, the house was used as a boarding school. W.H. Butler bought the estate at the end of the 1860s, when it was described as comprising of twenty-nine acres. The grounds included extensive greenhouses, a vinery, coach house and even a farmhouse.

Frederick Pickles, a highly respected headmaster of St George School January 1895 to July 1929. He was courteous and firm and expected his staff to have the same virtues. He was instrumental in establishing the school's good reputation.

Nine
Leisure and Life

East Bristol has through the years reflected the many changes in British society. The Church was very prominant, the area had and still has many pubs. The Park since 1894 has held a unique position in people's affections. The schools of the district hopefully provided a positive springboard and friends. A rich tapestry of people, events, organizations and places have all made their mark on the community. A vibrant world of laughter, fun, fantasy and adventure was provided by the areas' three cinemas.

The Park cinema was built in 1911. It was Bristol's ninth cinema and it was built on land between the Three Horseshoes and one of the entrances to St George Park. The first cinemascope film in Bristol was shown here by owner Sydney Gamlin, who also owned the Cabot and Van Dyke cinemas. The Park cinema closed because of a love story. The manager was having an affair with an usherette and Mr Gamlin took a very serious view of this and warned them to stop. They didn't or couldn't and he sacked them and closed the cinema in 1964. It was demolished three years later. On seeing it being pulled down and old man watching, commented that it cost £900 to build and £2,500 to knock down. Today the site is an empty grass space with a few trees.

The Granada cinema opened in 1912 and was then known as the St George Hall Electric Palace. At that time it was situated in Victoria Road (later Victoria Parade). In 1927 the Pugsley family bought it and made it a very grand cinema seating 750 people. An impressive entrance was made on Church Road and later its name was changed to the Granada. It closed as a cinema in December 1961 and the last film it showed was The Alamo. The building was then used for bingo for many years. In 1998 it was converted into a Wetherspoons pub which was called St Georges Hall, reflecting its cinema past.

A revival of days past in St George Park in 1990s.

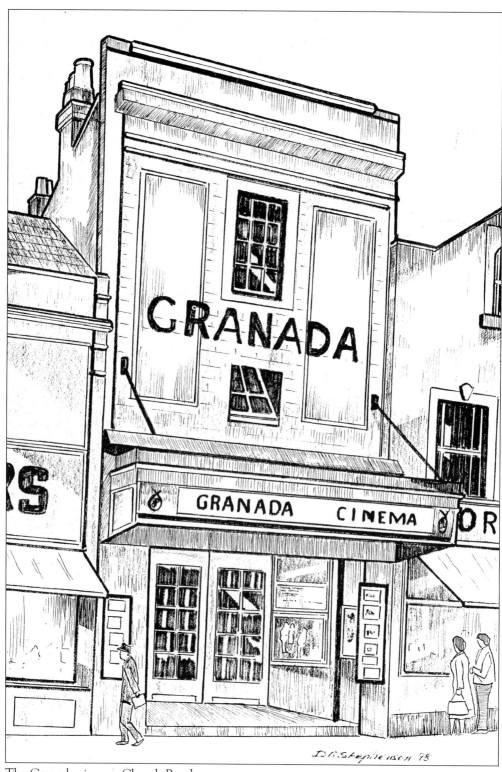

The Granada cinema, Church Road.

The Park Cinema, Church Road. Off to the right is a footpath leading into St George Park.

The Kingsway Cinema on Two Mile Hill Road. Opened in 1928, it was described then as a 'handsome stone-faced cinema'. It cost £9,000 and seated 800. It closed in 1959 and all of its fourteen employees were sacked. The structure then became a car showroom, which remains in use today.

Croft End Mission Silver Band, August 1926. Crofts End Mission, near Deep Pit, was founded in 1895. Like other such bodies, it provided a positive fellowship for workers and their families. Concerts, choirs, bands and Sunday schools were all part of the picture.

Redfield United Front supporters at Packers Ground, Whitehall at Whitsuntide. This large sports ground had once been the site of two market gardens: Johnson's fields were the original western section and to the east were Gerrish's market gardens which stretched up to Johnny Crow's Lane (now Gordon Road). Both were purchased by the Packers Chocolate firm for a recreation ground.

Whitehall Pavilion which was built and named after Mr C. Bruce Cole, owner of Packers. During the First World War the pavilion was home to Belgian refugees. It was originally much more ornate. It was acquired for St George School and in the 1930s, was used for art, woodwork and cookery as well as for changing rooms.

John Williams and Ernie Fortune, English bowls champions in 1931. St George had its own bowls club, which was very successful and these were two of its champions. John only had one eye after an accident but this did not stop him winning this beautiful cup.

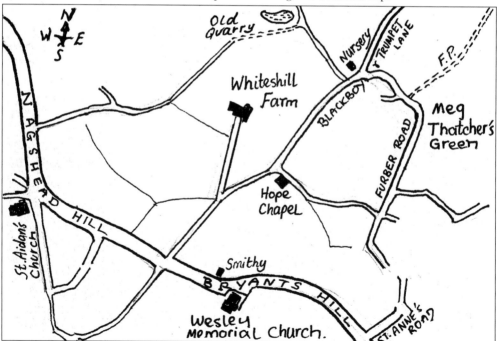

A 1920s map showing St George towards Hanham. The Wesley Memorial Church (centre bottom) was opened in 1907 on land provided by Mr Furber. The Hope Chapel (centre) is situated in the middle of fields and lanes; the Kingsway and associated roads which are now located here were constructed later. Meg Thatcher's Green (right) is a place name that probably dates back to before the fifteenth century.

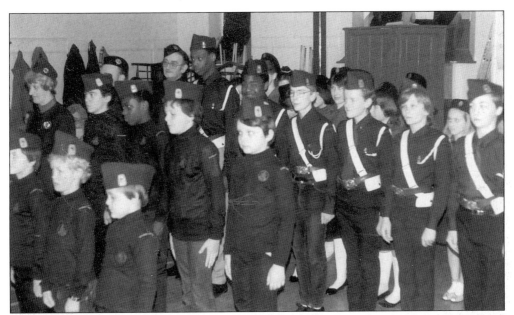

A joint 36th Boys Brigade and 99th Girl Guide display evening at Bethesda Sunday School room in the 1980s. The 99th Guides Company was founded in 1929 and was attached to Redfield Methodist. In the mid-1970s the 99th transferred to its present home at Bethesda.

The united churches of Bristol East, annual procession on Whit Sunday, 1967. They have just passed the Kingsway, threading towards Kingswood. A time of colourful banners and brass bands.

The May festival at St Matthew Moorfields, Church Road, 1930s. This view is looking across Church Road to the Co-op funeral and masonry site. In the 1950s a new funeral parlour and chapel of rest were built in front of the garage. The complex was further extended when, sadly, the Masons Arms was pulled down.

Mr and Mrs Thomas Butler, owners of Butlers Tar Works, and their friends in their 1904 Clement. Numberplates were introduced from 1 January 1904 and AE1 was Bristol's first number plate. It now adorns the Bristol Lord Mayor's official car.

A tipper truck owned by C. Harding and Sons who were haulage contractors situated at 74 Bell Hill Road. In the 1920s petrol driven vehicles replaced horse-drawn vehicles, which were still the mainstay of many local hauliers and coal merchants, and were a great step forward. (JW)

A steam roller belonging to Buckinghamshire County Council working for Bristol Corporation at Whitehall Road near the Beaufort Arms public house in the early 1920s.

Tramcar No. 158 at St George Fountain. It is seen in 1940 in wartime livery on the Kingswood route with blackout shaded windows and white fenders and truck sides.

112

St George tram depot, Beaconsfield Road in the 1930s. In 1876 Bristol Tramways Co. Ltd opened its eastbound line between Old Market and St George. Note the inscription 'Bristol Tramways 1876' and the large notice boards.

A view of St George tram depot taken on 12 August 1987 when demolition was in progress.

St George police station on the corner of Church Road and Northcote Road was opened in 1881. It replaced the previous police station which was located on the corner of Church Road and Blackswarth Road (where Lloyds TSB Bank is today). The building was quite large and boasted its own stables at the rear. It closed in 1998 and was converted into private flats.

Bristol St George FC. The club was formed on 24 October 1882 and is Bristol's oldest. The club turned professional in 1896 but reverted back to amateur status in 1900. Bristol St George FC has won many cups and trophies over the years and this picture shows the triumphant team that won the Gloucestershire Senior Amateur Cup in 1953. The club, now named Roman Glass, St George, still play at Bell Hill, where home games have been played since 1896.

Opposite: St George Fire Station. In 1899 a new fire station was built to the rear of the police station in Northcote Road. St George Volunteer Fire Brigade was then disbanded and replaced by Bristol Police Fire Brigade, financed by Bristol Corporation. The station closed in 1939 but was reopened in 1939 as an AFS station. It then became an NFS station in 1941 and was finally closed for good in 1948. It was converted into flats, with the police station, in 1998.

Charlie Heal's funfair. The great Bristol showman Charlie Heal presented fairs in St George Park for over fifty years. His son, Charlie Heal Jnr, is said to have been born in the Park in 1901. Charlie Heal travelled with roundabouts and amusements which were hauled by great steam engines like this Burrel, No. 2804, which was named *The White Rose of York*. Other engines were named *His Majesty* and *Her Majesty*.

Charlie Heal's fair organ. In the early part of the century, popular rides were the Golden Gallopers and Switchbacks, all powered by steam. Music was supplied by loud colourful organs with moving figures, like this eighty-nine-key example belonging to Charlie Heal. Charlie had great affection for the park and owned a house facing the park in Lyndale Road, where he lived with his second wife.

George Roger's Motorcycle Speedway. In the 1930s new faster rides were seen at the park, such as the Dodgems and Speedway. As well as rides belonging to the Heal family, rides belonging to other showman appeared occasionally. This magnificent motorcycle speedway ride was owned by George Rogers and Sons. In later years other rides to be seen were the chair-o-planes, dive bomber, rotor, ghost train, big wheel and shows such as the wall of death and of course boxing booths.

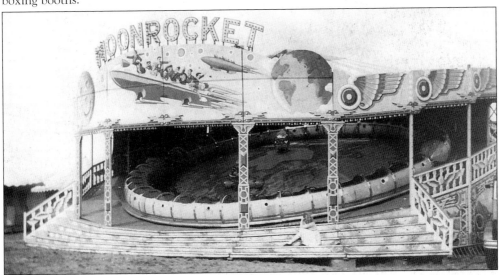

Charlie Heal's Moonrocket. During the Second World War, the government allowed showmen to open their amusements in local parks under a scheme called 'Holidays at Home'. The fairs were held at St George Park, on the hard ground where the skateboard park is now built. The best remembered ride from the war years and the 1950s was the 'Moonrocket'. It was a very fast circular ride which also featured an effigy of Popeye riding on a rocket. The fairs in St George Park stopped in the mid-to late 1950s.

Mr Perrott, gardener at Summerhill House, standing outside of the Grapehouse in the 1930s. The estate was situated just to the west of Marling Road.

An early charabanc trip to Ilfracombe from St George. Foss, wearing XIV cap, is seen in the centre of the picture. George Foss was the son of Dr Edwin Foss who lived at Summerhill House.

In 2000, alterations to 136 Church Road uncovered the wording 'Challenge Stores', not seen since the 1930s. In the 1950s, 136 was Bressingtons greengrocers. Next door was Dicks grocery store.

William Gray outside his shop in Bell Hill Road (see p.54)

The 1894 staff at St George Higher Grade School.

A view of the lower hall and science block extension of Rose Green School taken from Thurstons Barton. Mrs Smith was headmistress of Rose Green Grammar School from 1952-1966. Mr A.E Francis was headmaster of St George Rose Green in the late 1970s.

The Prince of Wales, an off-licence situated in Gordon Road just before the junction with Gordon Avenue. The side wall display windows and door were added in the 1950s. The building was subsequently demolished to make way for new houses.

The Horse and Jockey, No. 56 Nag's Head Hill. To the east were lanes leading to Whiteshill Farm, Meg Thatcher's Green and Magpie Bottom. Market gardening was carried out at Magpie Bottom, a small valley lying between St George and Hanham.

Kath Rees and her brother Edward in St George Park in 1937. St George School is in the background.

A young Doreen Parsons (*née* Sheeley) with her uncle Tom in St George Park in 1938. St Ambrose Church is in the background.

Crews Hole, an early Victorian Methodist chapel, dating from 1853. The building is adjoined by school rooms as was common practice at the time.

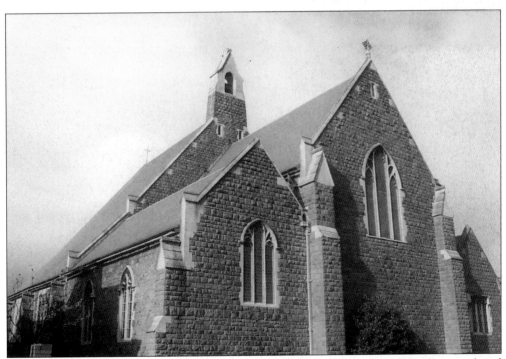

St Aidan, Nicholas Lane, which opened 1 October 1904. The design, by G.F. Bodley, was based on an interpretation of a fourteenth century church in the free gothic revival style.

Whitehall Tavern, on the corner of
Devon Road and Saffron Street.
This popular pub survived the
demolition of the street in the late
1960s.

D.G. STEPHENSON

Drawing of a 1950s/60s type
publican.

The plaque commemorating the work of Whitefield and John and Charles Wesley which is located on Whitehall Road, the former site of Rose Green School.

An evocative shot of Troopers Hill, looking towards St Aidan's Church.

A representation of the 1845 Tithe
Map of the parish of St George.

About the Authors

Andy Jones has been Chairman of Barton Hill History Group since 1991. A native of Redfield, his early interest in history was prompted by Ladybird books, Airfix and Whitehall School (Mrs Hemming and Miss Chelmicka). He first became interested in local history while at Rose Green School (St George Comprehensive). He acknowledges Mr Smith and Mr Crouch, history teachers at Rose Green and St George Upper School, for significantly encouraging and developing his interest in history. Also influential was the local history section of St George Library. Andy has written many items for the BHHG's magazine *The Bartonian* plus numerous articles which have been published in local newspapers. He has also contributed to local history videos and books.

David Cheesley was born and bred in East Bristol and was educated at Whitehall and then Speedwell School. In 1974 he became interested in family history and succeeded in tracing his family tree directly back to 1733. This in turn took him onto local history and the Barton Hill History Group. He has been secretary since the beginning and has written many articles for the Group's magazine, *The Bartonian*, and co-written many of the Group's books. In 1987 he wrote *War on the Hill*, the wartime history of Barton Hill, and in 1998 *Bristol Transport* with Tempus Publishing, which included over 200 photographs from his collection of road and rail transport. As well as writing and researching books he enjoys producing and presenting slide shows on a variety of local history topics and has also been involved in the production of three videos, *Barton Hill*, *St George*, and *Railways of Bristol*.

David Stephenson was born in Bloy Street, Easton. His father was a projectionist at the Globe and Granada cinemas. His parents met and courted in this area. David bought his first house in Cossham Road, St George when he got married, so he has always known these streets well. He wrote *The History of Lawrence Hill* as a member of the Barton Hill History Group. He also helped to write and produce a book and video of Barton Hill.
With Andy Jones, Dave Cheesley and Tony Brake he wrote and produced the video on St George, Redfield and Whitehall and has written many articles for the *Bristol Evening Post*. He has also worked on local history theatre including *Yesterday's Island*, *The Day War Broke Out in Bristol*, *You've Never Had It So Good* and he recently appeared in the Bristol Old Vic production of *Up the Feeder and Down the Mouth*.

Jill Willmott (*née* Payne) was brought up in St George, attending Summerhill and Speedwell Schools and her husband Paul Willmott is from Cock Road, Kingswood. They have written four books on Kingswood and have collected photographs and ephemera relating to the area and for many years their collection has been used in many local videos and publications.

If you enjoyed this book and have photographs, documents and memories, newspaper cuttings etc of the area the Barton Hill History Group would be pleased to see them. Please contact:

David Stephenson
7 New Cheltenham Road
Kingswood
Bristol
BS15 1TH